GET THE ANSWERS! History

Q&A ABOUT THE JAMESTOWN COLONY

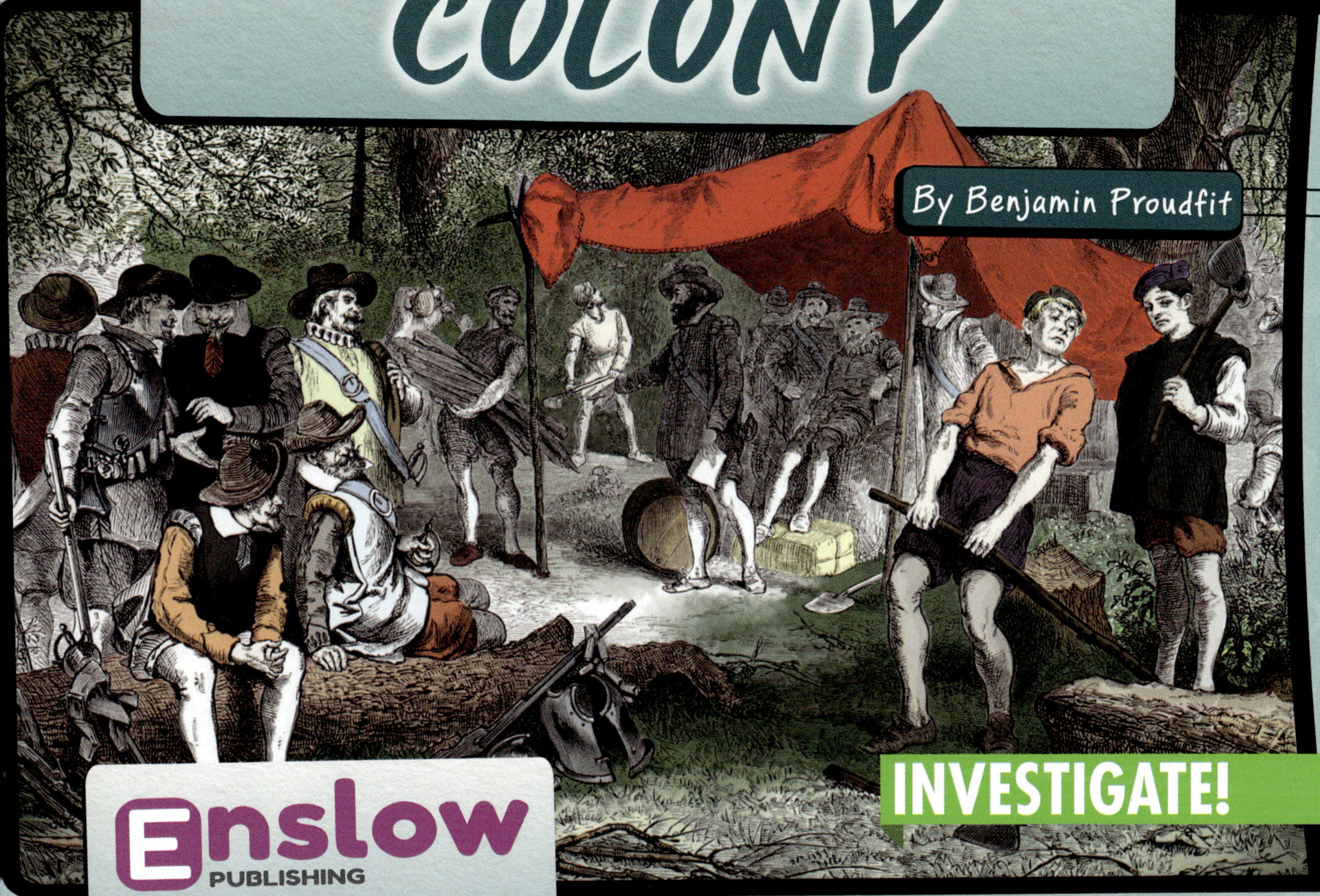

By Benjamin Proudfit

INVESTIGATE!

Enslow PUBLISHING

Please visit our website, www.enslow.com. For a free color catalog of all our high-quality books, call toll free 1-800-398-2504 or fax 1-877-980-4454.

Library of Congress Cataloging-in-Publication Data

Names: Proudfit, Benjamin, author.
Title: Q & A about the Jamestown Colony / Benjamin Proudfit.
Other titles: Questions and answers about the Jamestown Colony
Description: Buffalo, New York : Enslow Publishing, 2026. | Series: Get the answers! History | Includes index. | Audience: Grades 2-3
Identifiers: LCCN 2024058621 (print) | LCCN 2024058622 (ebook) | ISBN 9781978544376 (library binding) | ISBN 9781978544369 (paperback) | ISBN 9781978544383 (ebook)
Subjects: LCSH: Jamestown (Va.)–History–17th century–Juvenile literature. | Virginia–History–Colonial period, ca. 1600-1775–Juvenile literature.
Classification: LCC F234.J3 P76 2026 (print) | LCC F234.J3 (ebook) | DDC 975.5/02–dc23/eng/20241218
LC record available at https://lccn.loc.gov/2024058621
LC ebook record available at https://lccn.loc.gov/2024058622

Published in 2026 by
Enslow Publishing
2544 Clinton Street
Buffalo, NY 14224

Designer: Andrea Davison-Bartolotta
Editor: Kristen Nelson

Photo credits: Cover, pp. 1, 13, 14, 20 The Miriam and Ira D. Wallach Division of Art, Prints and Photographs: Picture Collection/NYPL Digital Collections; series art (question mark backgrounds) Darcraft/Shutterstock.com; pp. 4–5 Eric Michael Teitelman/Shutterstock.com; p. 5 File:The Generall Historie of Virginia, New-England, and the Summer Isles by Captain John Smith.jpg/Wikimedia Commons; pp. 6, 10 Library of Congress; pp. 7, 24 Internet Archive Book Images/Flickr.com; pp. 8, 19 (inset) Joseph Sohm/Shutterstock.com; p. 9 (main) File:VirginiaCompanyArms JohnStowSurveyOfLondon 1632.PNG/Wikimedia Commons; p. 9 (frame) BearFotos/Shutterstock.com; p. 11 Zack Frank/Shutterstock.com; p. 12 Rosenwald Collection/National Gallery of Art; p. 15 Morphart Creation/Shutterstock.com; p. 16 Christine_Kohler/iStockphoto.com; p. 17 North Wind Picture Archives/Alamy Stock Photo; p. 18 Timothy L Barnes/Shutterstock.com; p. 19 (main) Sean Pavone/Shutterstock.com; p. 21 (title) MIKHAIL GRACHIKOV/Shutterstock.com; p. 21 (true/false buttons) baldezh/Shutterstock.com; pp. 22, 23 Everett Collection/Shutterstock.com; p. 25 Library of Virginia; p. 26 John Couture/Shutterstock.com; p. 27 Anadolu_Dizgi/Shutterstock.com; p. 28 NASA/GSFC/Lawrence Ong, EO-1 Mission Science Office; p. 29 (bottom) hutch photography/Shutterstock.com; p. 29 (top) Sean Pavone/Shutterstock.com.

Printed in the United States of America

CPSIA compliance information: Batch #CS26ENS: For further information contact Enslow Publishing, at 1-800-398-2504.

CONTENTS

Words in the glossary appear in **bold** type the first time they are used in the text.

LOOK BACK AT JAMESTOWN

Jamestown is one of the most important settlements in American history! However, it had a rocky start. Illness and hunger killed many of the first settlers. Contact with nearby Native American groups was sometimes friendly and sometimes not. The conditions in Jamestown got so bad the colonists even tried to **abandon** it at one point!

Even today, historians study what was left behind by those who lived at Jamestown in those early years. Hundreds of years later, there's still more to learn!

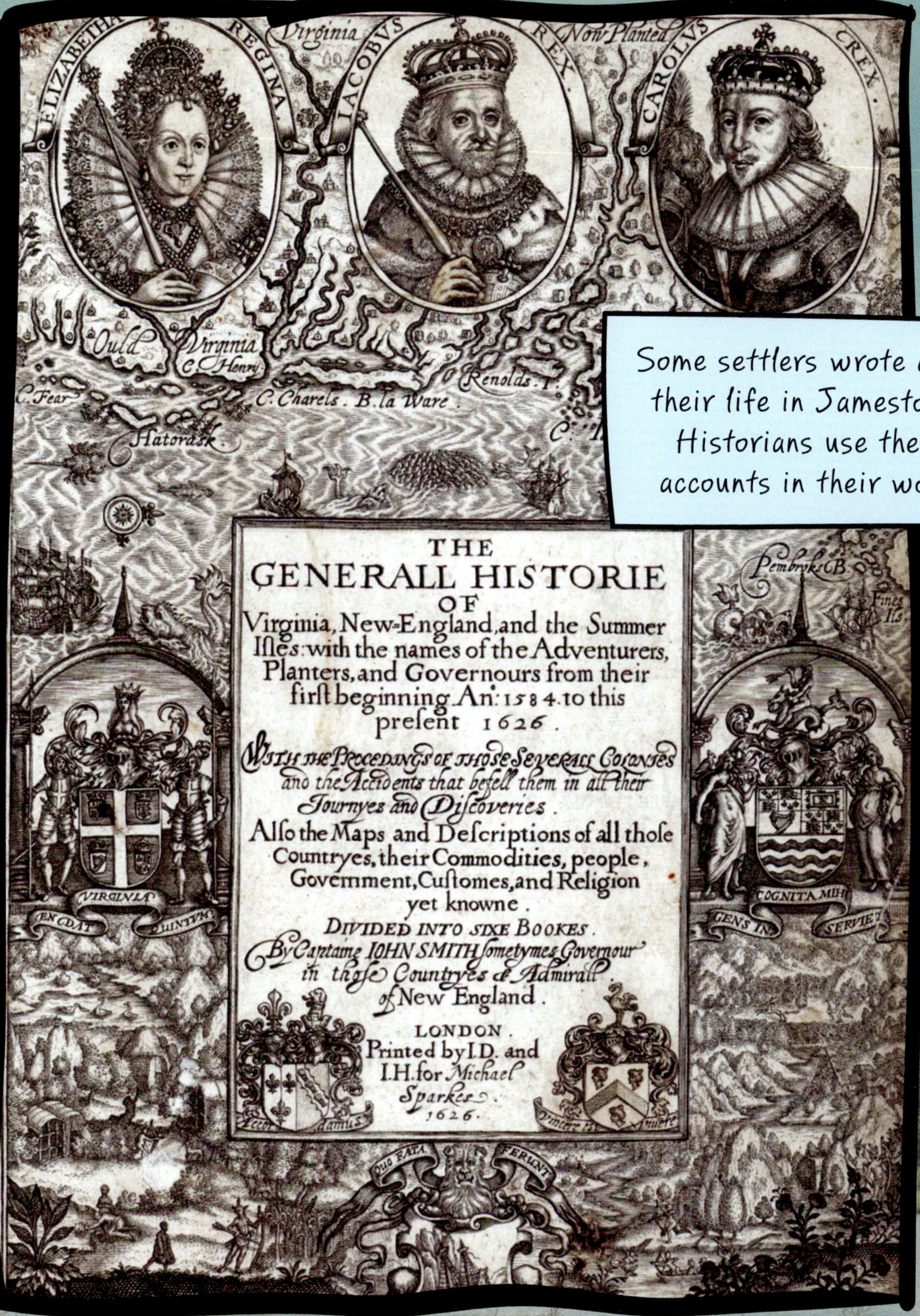

THE
GENERALL HISTORIE
OF
Virginia, New-England, and the Summer Isles: with the names of the Adventurers, Planters, and Governours from their first beginning An: 1584. to this present 1626.

With the Procedings of those Severall Colonies and the Accidents that befell them in all their Journyes and Discoveries.

Also the Maps and Descriptions of all those Countryes, their Commodities, people, Government, Customes, and Religion yet knowne.

DIVIDED INTO SIXE BOOKES.

By Captaine IOHN SMITH sometymes Governour in those Countryes & Admirall of New England.

LONDON.
Printed by I.D. and I.H. for Michael Sparkes.
1626.

Some settlers wrote about their life in Jamestown. Historians use these accounts in their work.

THE FIRST WHAT?

QUESTION 1

Was Jamestown the first colony in North America?

ANSWER

No. Both the French and Spanish built settlements in present-day Florida in the 1560s. The Spanish soon pushed the French out. Their colony of St. Augustine grew to be the longest continuously **inhabited** settlement begun by Europeans in the United States.

St. Augustine was founded in 1565.

QUESTION 2

Was Jamestown the first British colony?

ANSWER

It wasn't! In 1587, British settlers founded the Roanoke Colony. The colony's leader left for England that same year to ask for more help and supplies. When he came back three years later, the settlement was empty!

No one knows for sure what happened to the Roanoke colonists. They disappeared!

QUESTION 3

Why was Jamestown important?

ANSWER

Jamestown was the first permanent British settlement. Permanent means long-lasting. Three ships set sail to found this colony in North America on December 6, 1606. They were called the *Susan Constant*, *Godpeed,* and *Discovery*.

These are replicas, or re-creations, of the three ships that sailed for Jamestown in 1606.

QUESTION 4

What was the Virginia Company?

ANSWER

Established in 1606 by the king of England, this company aimed to colonize a certain part of North America. It also planned to make money while doing that! Later, it had a part in setting up the government of the colony of Virginia.

coat of arms of the Virginia Company

QUESTION 5

How did they pick the place to settle?

ANSWER

The Virginia Company told the settlers to choose a place that was surrounded by water on three sides. This made it easier to **protect** the settlement from the Spanish, should they attack. There were also places in the nearby water deep enough to keep British ships.

The settlers arrived in Virginia in May 1607. They established their colony at the mouth of the James River.

QUESTION 6

Was it a good idea to settle in that spot?

ANSWER

Not really. The land was **swampy** and not good for growing crops. The James River that ran next to the newly built fort did not offer good drinking water.

Historic Jamestowne

QUESTION 7

Why did they call it Jamestown?

ANSWER

The colonists named the settlement after the British king, James I. He ruled England from 1603 to 1625. James I was also the king of Scotland at the time, though he was King James VI there.

James I

The Jamestown settlement had many names over the early years, including James Forte, James Towne, and James Cittie.

QUESTION 8

Who were the Jamestown settlers?

ANSWER

About 105 men and boys came to Jamestown at first. Forty of them were soldiers. Some came to be workmen or do certain jobs, such as blacksmithing. Around 35 of the new settlers were gentlemen, or those from the upper classes.

One problem the Jamestown colony faced was the gentlemen colonists wouldn't do work they didn't want to do.

HARD TIMES

QUESTION 9

Who were the Native groups nearby?

ANSWER

The Powhatan were a group of about 30 tribes that lived around the Jamestown Colony. Their leader was named Wahunsenacawh. The settlers called him Chief Powhatan. The Powhatan attacked the colony at times and helped it at others.

Wahunsenacawh

QUESTION 10

Did Jamestown succeed right away?

ANSWER

No! The colonists got sick within months of arriving from unhealthy water and illness carried by mosquitoes, among other reasons. Many died. New colonists came in 1608. But then a fire burned down some of the settlement.

Instead of working to better the colony, many Jamestown colonists spent their time looking for gold.

QUESTION 11

Who was John Smith?

ANSWER

Smith first took over as leader of Jamestown in 1608. He tried to turn the settlement around. He said, "He who will not work shall not eat." However, he was forced out of his job, and he went back to England.

John Smith

QUESTION 12

What was the "starving time"?

ANSWER

During the winter of 1609, the colonists barely left the settlement for fear of being attacked by the Powhatans. They quickly ran out of food and ate anything they could, including shoe leather. Most of them died by early 1610.

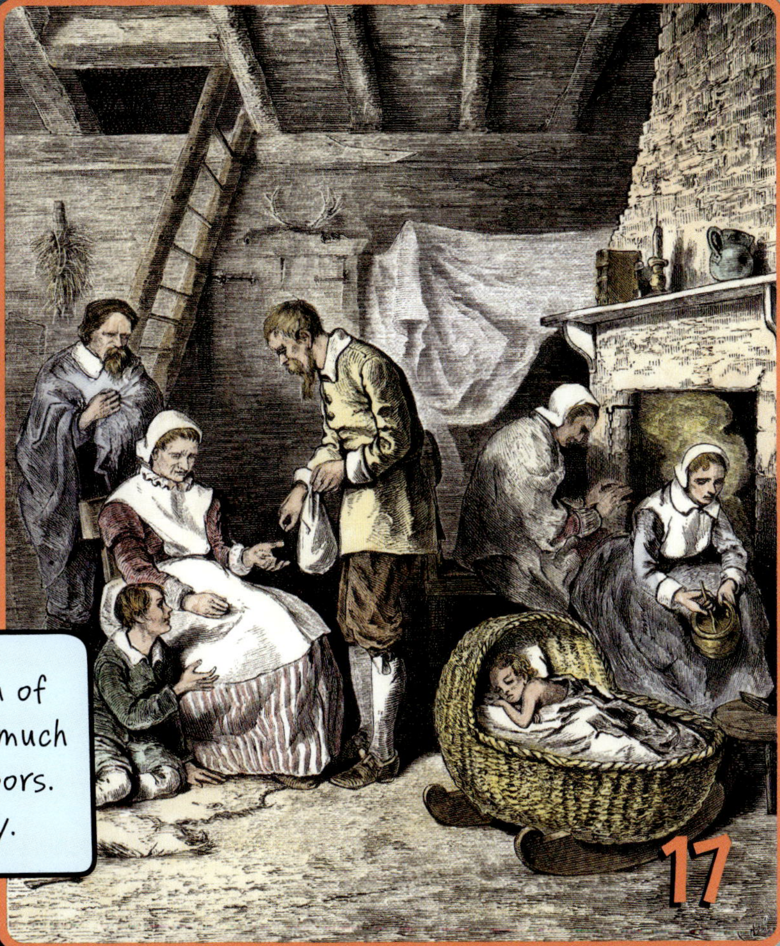

By the end of 1609, the men of Jamestown had asked for too much food from their Native neighbors. The Powhatans were angry.

QUESTION 13

Did they almost abandon the colony?

ANSWER

Yes! New settlers came to Jamestown in 1610 and found a struggling colony. They all decided to leave and return to England. As they were sailing away, they met three Virginia Company ships in Chesapeake Bay. Their leader—Lord Delaware, Thomas West—made the Jamestown group go back! He had brought 150 new settlers.

If the colonists had left, people wouldn't be visiting the historic Jamestown Settlement today!

Jamestown Settlement

POCAHONTAS

QUESTION 14

What did Pocahontas have to do with Jamestown?

ANSWER

Pocahontas was Chief Powhatan's daughter. She was **kidnapped** in 1613. The Jamestown colonists wanted Powhatan to free English prisoners and give back arms and tools. He freed the prisoners but wouldn't give anything back. Pocahantas was not freed.

Pocahontas

TRUE OR FALSE

POCAHONTAS WAS A TEENAGER WHEN JAMESTOWN WAS SETTLED.

FALSE

She would have been a child of about 11. She was born around 1596.

POCAHONTAS SAVED JOHN SMITH'S LIFE.

POSSIBLY **FALSE**

Smith wrote that Pocahontas saved his life when he was taken by the Powhatan. Many historians don't think she would have been present at the times he writes about, but it's hard to know for sure!

POCAHONTAS WAS A PEACEMAKER.

TRUE

Sending the chief's favorite daughter with other Powhatans to visit Jamestown showed the settlers the meeting was peaceful.

POCAHONTAS LATER BECAME KNOWN AS REBECCA.

TRUE

Pocahontas became a **Christian** and married an Englishman. She started using a new name.

See how some of the stories you may have heard about Pocahontas check out!

QUESTION 15

Who was John Rolfe?

ANSWER

Rolfe married Pocahontas in 1614. This brought peace between the settlers and the Powhatan for many years. Even more importantly, Rolfe was the first to plant a certain kind of tobacco. It became so successful that other colonists did it too.

Tobacco growing became a big part of the Virginia **economy**.

IN 1619

QUESTION 16

Did slavery start in Jamestown?

ANSWER

No, slavery is a practice that had happened around the world for hundreds of years. But historians often trace slavery in North America to 1619 in Jamestown. That year, the first recorded ship of **enslaved** Africans came to the settlement.

Traveling from Africa to North America took four to six weeks. Enslaved people faced terrible conditions and had little food and water on the journey.

QUESTION 17

When did women come to live in Jamestown?

ANSWER

By 1619, about 100 women lived in Jamestown. They came on some of the ships of settlers. But, in 1619 alone about 90 women sailed to the colony. They were meant to start families to live and grow in the colony.

QUESTION 18

What was the House of Burgesses?

ANSWER

By 1619, other settlements had grown up near Jamestown. That year, the Virginia Company set up the House of Burgesses, the first **representative** government body in the colonies. Its job was to pass laws and establish some order in the Virginia settlements.

The House of Burgesses lasted as Virginia's government until 1776, shortly before the United States declared independence from England.

BECOMING A COLONY

QUESTION 19

When did Virginia become a royal colony?

ANSWER

By the 1620s, the Virginia Company and King James weren't getting along. In 1624, King James broke up the Virginia Company. Virginia, and Jamestown with it, became a colony under his power.

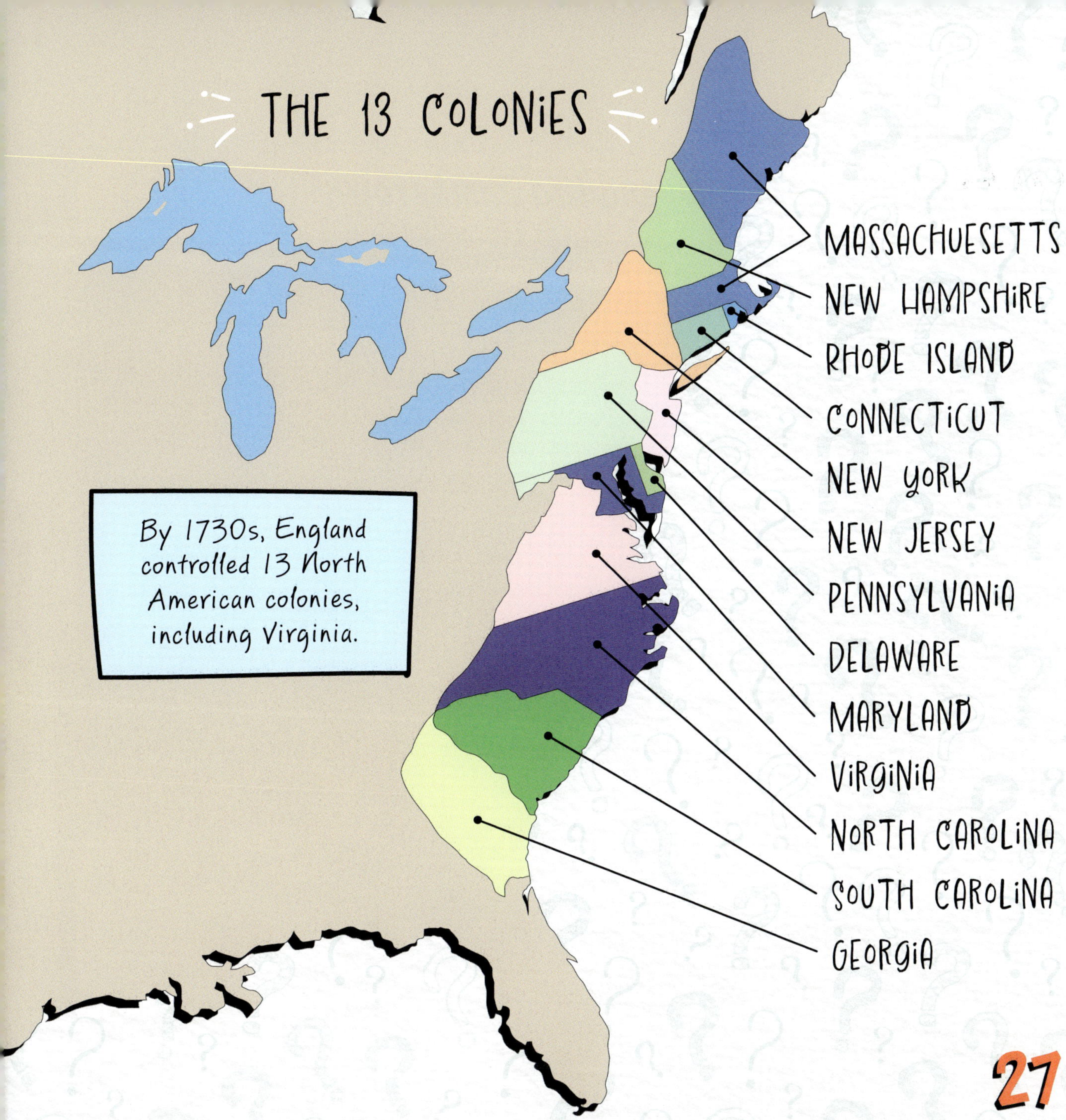

By 1730s, England controlled 13 North American colonies, including Virginia.

QUESTION 20

What happened to Jamestown?

ANSWER

Jamestown was the capital city of Virginia until 1698. That year, the statehouse burned down. Williamsburg became the new capital. The **peninsula** Jamestown was on began to disappear too. Today, this land is an island!

The land that was Jamestown is now protected by the government of Virginia and National Park Service.

Jamestown Island, satellite view

Williamsburg, Virginia today

Historic Jamestowne

GLOSSARY

abandon: To leave empty or uncared for.

Christian: Follower of Jesus Christ.

economy: The money made in an area and how it is made.

enslaved: Having to do with being owned by another person and forced to work without pay under terrible conditions.

inhabit: To live in a place.

kidnap: Taken against one's will.

peninsula: A narrow piece of land that extends into water from the mainland.

protect: To keep safe.

representative: Having to do a government in which the people are represented by those who are elected to their position.

satellite: An object that circles Earth in order to collect and send information or aid in communication.

swampy: Having to do with an area with trees that is covered with water at least part of the time.

FOR MORE INFORMATION

BOOKS

Connors, Kathleen. *Q & A About Colonial America*. Buffalo, NY: Enslow Publishing, 2025.

Freeburg, Jessica. *A Jamestown Colony Time Capsule: Artifacts of the Early American Colony*. North Mankato, MN: Capstone Press, 2021.

Hansen, Grace. *Living in Colonial America*. Minneapolis, MN: Pop!, 2024.

WEBSITES

Colonial America
https://www.ducksters.com/history/colonial_america/
Find out about how the North American colonies were founded.

Historic Jamestowne
https://historicjamestowne.org/
You can visit Historic Jamestowne and learn all about the first permanent English colony!

INDEX